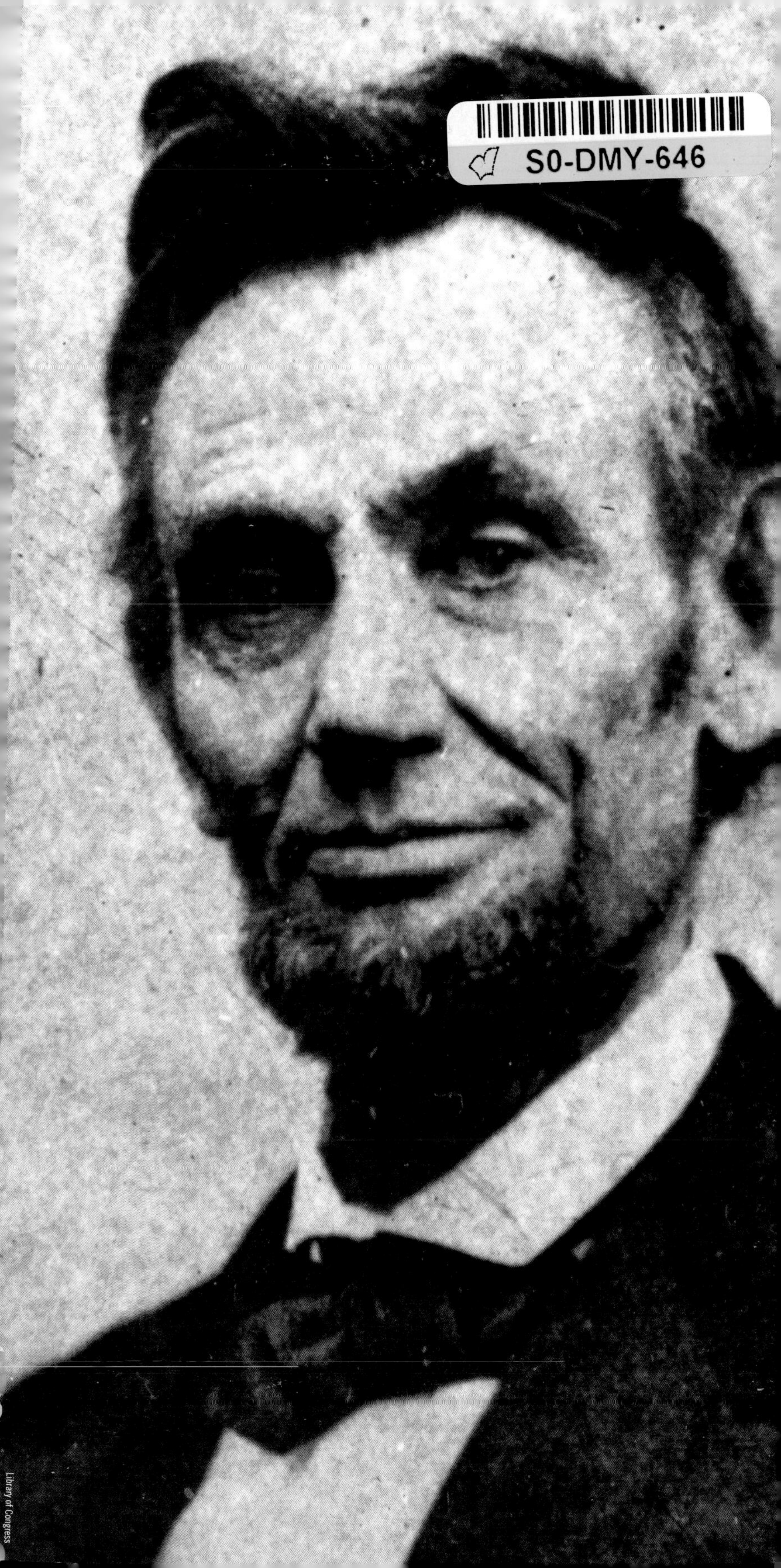

Library of Congress

ISBN NO. 1-57427-124-5

Distributed by Howell Press
1713-2D Allied Lane
Charlottesville, VA 22903
www.howellpress.com

Printed by Finlay Printing, Bloomfield, CT
Design by side view/Hannah Smotrich

Civil War to Civil Rights

Washington's Downtown Heritage Trail

by Richard T. Busch

With an Introduction
by Kathryn Schneider Smith
Executive Director
DC Heritage Tourism Coalition

HOWELL PRESS
Charlottesville, Virginia

*As you walk this trail,
please keep safety
in mind, just as you
would while visiting
any unfamiliar place.*

TABLE OF CONTENTS

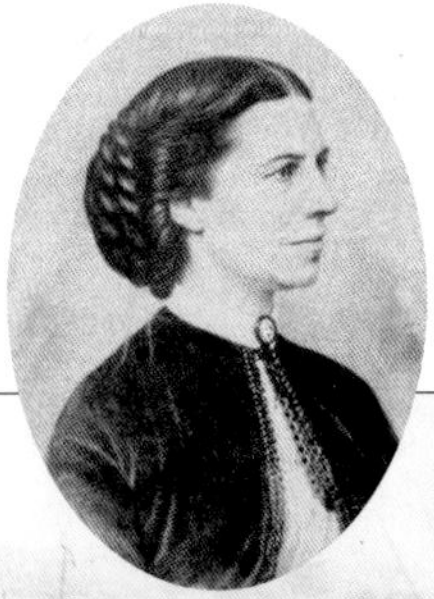
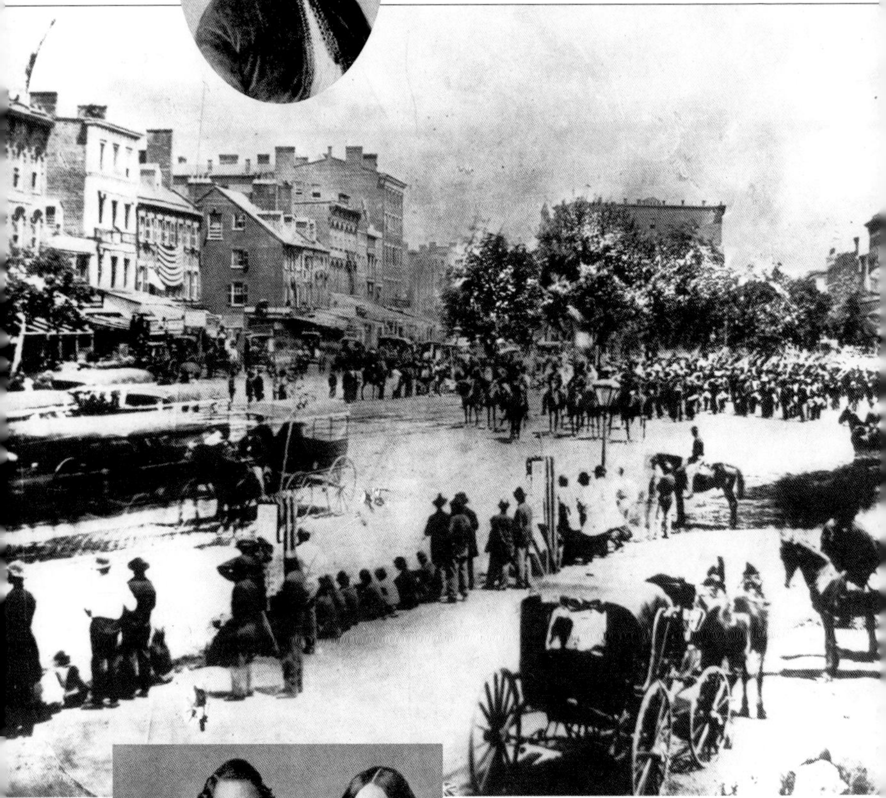
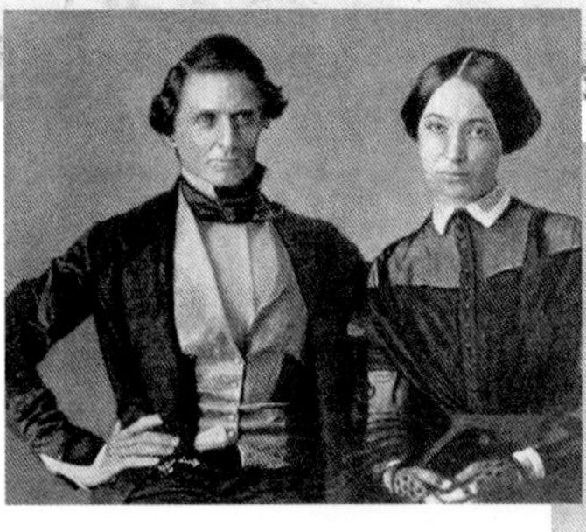
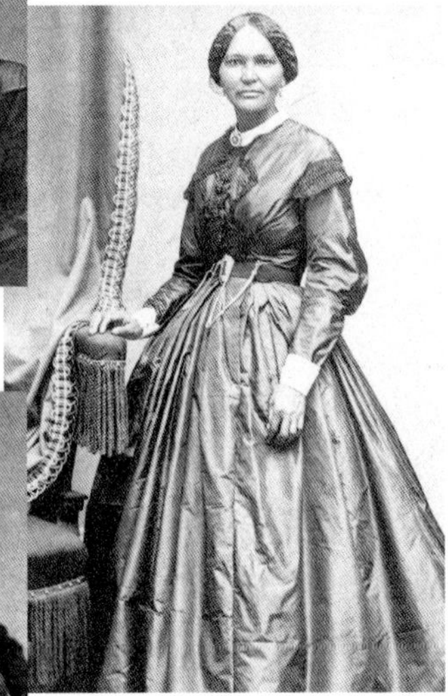
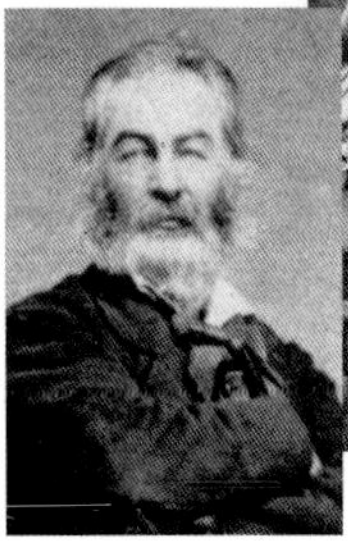

Introduction

DOWNTOWN WASHINGTON, D.C., is rich in little-known historic sites where you can touch and feel the American past. We have chosen to focus on two pivotal themes that link the history of the city with that of the nation —the Civil War and the continuing challenge to realize the American dream of equal rights for all its citizens.

Boston, for many visitors, represents our colonial and Revolutionary War history with its Freedom Trail. Philadelphia, with the Liberty Bell and Independence Hall, tells the story of the creation of the new nation. Washington, D.C., in turn, has been at the heart of the struggle to preserve the Union and fulfill its promise.

Downtown Washington, D.C., still echoes with the footsteps of Abraham Lincoln, Clara Barton, Walt Whitman, Frederick Douglass, African Americans seeking freedom, and the hundreds of thousands of soldiers and citizens who flooded the city between 1860 and 1865. After the war, the city emerged from a muddy backwater town to the grand capital envisioned by George Washington. The Civil War was the crucial event in the history of the city, which for the first time became a true center of national power, and the symbol of America's democratic ideals. ➤

The struggle for civil rights has also been central to the history of the city. A newspaper published in downtown Washington, the *National Era,* serialized a work by an unknown author, Harriet Beecher Stowe. It was called *Uncle Tom's Cabin.* Lincoln freed District slaves eight months before the Emancipation Proclamation freed slaves in the rebellious states. Howard University law students and professors, among them Thurgood Marshall, created the strategies and supported the picket lines that led to the end of racial segregation. It was at the Willard Hotel in downtown Washington that Martin Luther King, Jr., put the finishing touches on his "I Have A Dream" speech that electrified and mobilized the nation. The trail will also lead you there.

Civil War and civil rights stand as bookends embracing more than a century of other stories about downtown D.C. The signs along the downtown heritage trail also celebrate the people from many nations who came to central Washington to seek an economic foothold. As shopkeepers and artisans, craftsmen and laborers, they left their stories behind in the buildings they built and the places where they worshipped. The trail signs also recognize the importance of downtown as a commercial

center, where millions flocked over the years by car and streetcar to patronize the department stores and small shops that lined Seventh and F Streets.

The path from the Civil War to civil rights has taken many turns. Today's Washingtonians are writing yet another chapter in the history of downtown. New museums and the MCI Center sports arena are joining new restaurants and shops to turn the heart of downtown Washington into a cultural and entertainment center. Today's visitor can not only enjoy these new attractions, but also savor, on this trail, the buildings, streets, and historic sites that remain to remind us of the rich legacy on which we build.

Kathryn Schneider Smith, Executive Director
DC Heritage Tourism Coalition

The Center Loop

IT TAKES ABOUT 60 MINUTES to walk the center loop of the downtown heritage trail along Seventh, F, and Tenth Streets and then back to Pennsylvania Avenue. This loop is the heart of the downtown trail. Along it you will see the building where Abraham Lincoln's second inaugural ball was held and the alley that was on John Wilkes Booth's escape route following his assassination of the president. You will also learn about Clara Barton's relief efforts for Union troops and similar efforts by Elizabeth Keckley on behalf of newly freed African Americans. On this loop you will stand in the area where the poet and Civil War nurse Walt Whitman stood as he watched a two-day victory parade of Union troops on Pennsylvania Avenue in May 1865. You may also visit Ford's Theatre and the Petersen House where Lincoln died. You will find coffee shops, restaurants, bookstores, and art galleries clustered on Seventh and nearby, and the U.S. Navy Memorial and Naval Heritage Center on Pennsylvania Avenue at Eighth Street.

.1 Market Space:
Yesterday's Town Square

.2 Ceremony at the Crossroads

.3 Clara Barton:
Angel of the Battlefield

.4 The Roots of Freedom
and Equality

.5 Abraham Lincoln
Walked Here

.6 John Wilkes Booth's Escape

.7 "Woodies" Comes to F Street

.8 Pennsylvania Avenue:
Main Street for the City
and the Nation

.1

SEVENTH AND PENNSYLVANIA AVENUE NW

Market Space: Yesterday's Town Square

President George Washington himself identified this area for use as a public market. In 1802, just two years after the federal government arrived from Philadelphia, the first buildings of the city's Center Market went up on the site now occupied by the National Archives. For the next 130 years, its presence made Seventh and Pennsylvania the city's town square.

Known early on as "Marsh Market" because of the marshy ground on which it stood, it attracted independent food vendors to both sides of Pennsylvania Avenue. Here, in the years before refrigeration, blacks and whites, African American slaves and freedmen, high government officials and working class men and women mingled on a daily basis to shop for meat, poultry, and produce from nearby farms in Virginia and Maryland, and for fish from the Potomac River.

By the time of the Civil War, this area was bustling with all kinds of commercial activity. Nearby was the Haymarket where you could buy feed for horses and cattle and catch a "hack," the horse-drawn taxi of the day. It was noisy and dusty, and when it rained, the whole place was a sea of mud. Before 1850, when slave trading became illegal in the District of Columbia, slave auctions took place at both the Haymarket and Center Market.

In 1870, the collection of ramshackle buildings and stalls that had housed the market for over half a century was demolished and replaced by the two-block-long, 60,000-square-foot new Center Market building designed by Adolph Cluss. The largest enclosed retail market in the

The Haymarket at the time of the Civil War.

Advertisement from an 1863 city directory. The Civil War was good for business in Washington and elsewhere.

A vendor at Center Market about 1890.

world, Center Market eventually housed over 1,000 vendors. It stretched two full blocks on Pennsylvania Avenue from Seventh to Ninth Streets until the 1930s, when it too was demolished to make way for the neo-classical National Archives building.

The poet Walt Whitman, a civilian volunteer from New York, very likely stopped at Marsh Market to buy small gifts for sick and wounded soldiers before making his rounds at makeshift Civil War army hospitals in the area. Whitman's presence remains in the area today with the words of his "Prayer of Columbus" carved in the granite wall at the foot of the escalator leading to the Archives Metro station. ➤

.1

Center Market, on the site of today's National Archives, in 1903.

National Archives
South side, Pennsylvania Avenue between Seventh and Ninth NW

This shrine houses our nation's most sacred documents — the Declaration of Independence, the Constitution, the Bill of Rights, and others — designed for their security and protection by John Russell Pope in 1935. Behind its impressive Corinthian colonnades and heroic sculptures are 22 tiers of storage, accessed from the Pennsylvania Avenue side of the building. The

Market Square, designed by Hartman-Cox architects and Morris Architects, in 1990.

ceremonial space at the top of a majestic staircase, where important documents are on display, is accessed from the National Mall side of the building. Hours: Daily 10 am to 5:30 pm

Cross Pennsylvania Avenue and walk to the center of the plaza on your left, the U.S. Navy Memorial.

U.S. Navy Memorial
North side, Pennsylvania Avenue at Eighth NW

The statue, "The Lone Sailor," located near the middle of the large granite map of the world, was designed by sculptor Stanley Bleifeld as part of the United States Navy Memorial and executed by Conklin Rossant Architects in 1987. The memorial honors all the men and women who have served in our country's sea services. The Naval Heritage Center in the building at 701 Pennsylvania Avenue NW, is open to the public.
Hours: Mondays–Saturdays: 9:30 am to 5:00 pm

The Market Square Complex
North side, Pennsylvania Avenue between Seventh and Ninth NW

Embracing Eighth Street at Pennsylvania Avenue is a pair of contemporary curved buildings (701 and 801 Pennsylvania Avenue) that reinforces the importance of this cross-street in Pierre L'Enfant's original plan for the city. Their design complements the neo-classical style of the 1930s Federal Triangle office-building complex and the National Archives across Pennsylvania Avenue. They contain a mix of uses, including residential units on the top floors.

▶ *Cross Seventh Street at the crosswalk just beyond the statue of Civil War Major General Winfield Scott Hancock, to the next trail sign. It's in front of the red-brick building with the golden dome.*

.2

Ceremony at the Crossroads

This intersection has been the crossroads of national ceremony and local commerce since the federal government located here 200 years ago. Pennsylvania Avenue has been the inaugural route for every United States president since Thomas Jefferson in 1801. Seventh Street developed as a commercial street from the city's beginnings. It was the primary artery for moving goods, linking farms in Maryland to the north with wharves on the Potomac River. During the Civil War, it was a major route for Union troops headed to Fort Stevens and other Civil War defenses north of the city, which were part of a ring of fortifications hurriedly built in 1861 to protect the capital from Confederate attack. In May 1865, a two-day-long parade of victorious Union troops passed this way along Pennsylvania Avenue to a White House review.

All around you today are reminders of the Civil War. However, looking toward Pennsylvania Avenue, the first thing you see is the graceful water-crane sculpture atop a small open temple in the plaza in front of the Riggs Bank. This is the Temperance Fountain designed and given to the city by Henry Cogswell of San Francisco in the 1880s. Created to promote the virtues of water over spirits, for many years it existed almost side by side with one of Washington's best-known liquor stores!

Behind the Temperance Fountain in the plaza is a memorial to Dr. Benjamin F. Stephenson, the founder of the Grand Army of the Republic, a national benevolent society established to assist Union veterans and widows of the fallen. It was dedicated in 1909 by a few hundred elderly veterans — a marked contrast to the thousands of Union troops who smartly paraded here in May 1865.

Sergeant Major Christian Fleetwood was awarded the Medal of Honor for heroism during the Civil War. He and other African American fighting troops were not allowed to march in the May 1865 victory parade because of General William Tecumseh Sherman's prejudice.

National Council of Negro Women
633 Pennsylvania Avenue NW

The building with the two conical towers on Pennsylvania Avenue was built as a hotel during the Civil War. Designed by prominent Washington architect Alfred Mullett, it later housed a bank, offices, and stores. In the 1980s it was renovated as part of the rejuvenation of the north side of Pennsylvania Avenue directed by the Pennsylvania Avenue Development Corporation. It is now the head-quarters of the National Council of Negro Women, Inc.

Mathew Brady's Studio

Around the corner on the upper floors of what was formerly 625–627 Pennsylvania Avenue (the pair of ornate four-story buildings next to the walkway), Civil War photographer Mathew Brady set up a studio. Brady worked here from 1858 until at least 1869 and won fame for his photographic portraits of important individuals of the day. His battle-field images brought the horror of the Civil War home to the American public. You can still see the north-facing studio windows at the back of the building's top floor. ➤

Mathew Brady as he looked in 1861, just after his return from photographing the Battle of Bull Run.

17

Richard Busch

Three of the oldest commercial buildings in Washington, D.C. stand at 637–641 Indiana Avenue.

.2

Riggs Bank
301 Seventh Street NW

The white stone building that faces the plaza was designed in 1889 for the National Bank of Washington. The massive character of its arches and columns, made of rough-cut granite, mark it as an example of the Richardsonian Romanesque style. In 1990, the rear wall of the bank was painted by Mame Cohalan with a *trompe l'oeil* ("fool the eye") image to make it look like the stone of the building's other three sides.

637–641 Indiana Avenue NW

These three 1820s buildings stood witness to the Civil War activity in this area and are among the best-preserved antebellum commercial structures in the city. Their low elevations, flat fronts, and gable roofs are characteristic of the Federal style. The building at 637 has the most intact façade. Inside is what may be the oldest operating elevator in the country, a model that the Otis Elevator Company displayed at a New York City exhibition in 1854.

Gallery Row, at 401–413 Seventh Street, illustrates how historic preservation and exemplary architecture complement each other and gives us a sense of how this street looked during the 19th century.

Richard Busch

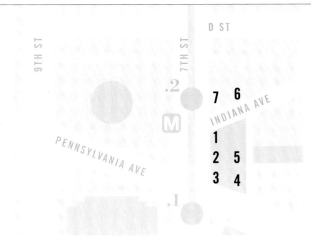

1 Temperance Fountain
2 GAR Memorial
3 National Council of Negro Women
4 Site of Mathew Brady's Studio
5 Trompe l'oeil (rear wall of Riggs Bank)
6 637–641 Indiana Avenue NW
7 Firemen's Insurance Building

Firemen's Insurance Company and National Union Insurance Company Buildings

Anchoring the corner of Seventh Street and Indiana Avenue are two red-brick 5- and 4-story buildings that represent the next stage of commercial building in this neighborhood. Designed in 1882, their bays, turrets, and golden dome identify them as a late-19th-century style called Queen Anne. Today, they have been incorporated into Liberty Place, a new office development designed in 1991 by Keyes Condon Florance, architects and Devrouax & Purnell, architects.

Walk up Seventh Street on the left-hand side. Note the group of buildings across the street at 401–413. Known as Gallery Row because of their current-day gallery use, they are, except for 413, examples of post-Civil War commercial structures designed in the Italianate style. Two distinguishing features are prominent window hoods and bracketed cornices. In 1986, Hartman-Cox, architects, and Mary Oehrlein & Associates, architects, restored the façades and placed new construction behind and between them at the same height as the original buildings, thus preserving the 19th-century scale of the streetscape.

❯ *Continue walking up Seventh to the next trail sign at number 437 on the right-hand side of the street. Clara Barton had her Civil War-era residence and office here.*

.3

Clara Barton: Angel of the Battlefield

In a sealed crawl space over the third floor of this building, a government employee named Richard Lyons made a startling discovery in 1997. Here, in a building scheduled for demolition, he found Civil War-era artifacts and documents, undisturbed for more than 100 years, that identified the structure as the office and residence of the famous Civil War nurse Clara Barton. From here, Barton organized independent battlefield relief efforts, and from here she searched for missing soldiers after the conflict was over. Thus to Barton's wartime humanitarian work can be added the title of the nation's first Missing In Action (MIA) investigator. This building is being preserved in her honor.

Barton came to Washington in 1854 from her native Massachusetts by way of New Jersey, where she had been a teacher. With the assistance of friends, she found a position as a clerk in the Patent Office. Such work was unusual for a woman at that time. A year later she was put in charge of the confidential desk, the first woman to receive a government service appointment. When the Civil War broke out Barton began organizing battlefield relief efforts by collecting donated medicine and other supplies and delivering them to the front.

Barton's battlefield heroics — bringing supplies to army doctors and nursing the wounded — earned her the title "Angel of the Battlefield." Her work took place in a war that saw over 600,000 combined Union and Confederate deaths, about as many American deaths as the total in all other wars in which the country has been involved.

MISSING SOLDIERS.
OFFICE. 3RD STORY, ROOM 9.
MISS CLARA BARTON.

This sign identified Clara Barton's Seventh Street office.

Clara Barton as she appeared at the time of the Civil War. Barton was 40 years old in 1861.

After the war, Barton took it upon herself to try to identify the graves of thousands of Union soldiers who died at Andersonville Confederate Prison in Georgia. Her success there led many people to write her requesting help locating loved ones. Barton located about 22,000 of the 62,000 missing soldiers and was eventually paid for her work by the federal government, in effect making her the first woman to head a federal office. She went on to found the American Red Cross in 1881.

While Barton was organizing medical relief and comfort for the Union wounded, Elizabeth Keckley, her African American contemporary, was doing the same for the growing community of former slaves flooding Washington. Born a slave herself, Keckley learned to sew at an early age and had become a highly professional seamstress by the time she was able to buy her freedom. ➤

.3

A portion of Mrs. Lincoln's letter to the president asking him to send a check for $200 to the Contraband Relief Society.

Keckley came to Washington, D.C., just before the Civil War, where, with the help of white clients, she became dressmaker to Varina Howell Davis, wife of Senator Jefferson Davis of Mississippi, who became president of the Confederacy. Jefferson Davis and his family left town when Mississippi seceded from the Union. Soon after the Lincolns arrived in 1861, Keckley became dressmaker to Mary Todd Lincoln.

Keckley saw the misery in which formerly enslaved African Americans, called "contrabands" by the federal government, were living. She created the Contraband Relief Society to provide clothing and education. In an 1862 letter to her husband, Mrs. Lincoln told him about Keckley's work and asked him to donate $200 to Keckley's society.

Elizabeth Keckley,
founder of the
Contraband Relief
Society and dressmaker
to the wives of
Washington's Civil
War power elite.

The Lansburgh
420–427 Seventh Street NW

Taking up much of the block across Seventh Street from Barton's office is the Lansburgh apartment building, which preserves elements of two smaller commercial buildings and the old Lansburgh Department Store. The complex, which now includes housing and the Shakespeare Theatre, was designed by Graham Gund Architects in 1991. The red band above the Art Deco façade on the southwest corner of Seventh and E is a clue to its original use — an S.S. Kresge Five and Dime.

Around the corner and down E Street, on the southeast corner with Eighth, is the main façade of the former Lansburgh Department Store, built in sections between 1916 and 1941. The exterior is made of molded and glazed terracotta (hard-fired clay) panels that could be reproduced for each expansion.

On your way up Seventh you will pass 501–507 and 509 Seventh Street, built respectively in 1868 and 1876, and altered in the first decade of the 20th century. These buildings represent the continuing commercialization of a block that was predominantly residential before the Civil War. Today this is an increasingly lively area of the city, filled with art galleries and restaurants.

❯ *Continue up Seventh Street to the corner of F Street, opposite the MCI Center, to the next trail sign.*

.4

SEVENTH AND F STREETS NW

The Roots of Freedom and Equality

The events that took place at or near this intersection are crucial to an understanding of slavery in the District of Columbia, the Civil War as it played out in the capital, and the continuing struggle for equality for all citizens of the United States.

The office and printing press of the *National Era,* an abolitionist newspaper, was located just north of the intersection of Seventh and F, where the MCI Center stands today. In April 1848, whites rioted here because they believed the newspaper had played a role in the attempted escape of 77 African American slaves from their District of Columbia owners aboard a ship named the *Pearl.* The whites wanted to destroy the press and possibly lynch the editor, Gamaliel Bailey.

The owner and crew of the ship had agreed to the night-time escape from a wharf on the Potomac. The vessel made it to the river's mouth when bad weather forced it to anchor near the shore. There the ship and its passengers were apprehended by a search party from Washington, tipped off by a spurned suitor whose lady had left him behind. The ship's captain and crew were tried, found guilty for stealing property, fined, and imprisoned. The escapees were quickly sold to a dealer in Alexandria. Ultimately, funds were collected and used to purchase the freedom of several slaves, including Mary Jane and Emily Catherine Edmonson. Descendants of the Edmonsons are today members of Asbury United Methodist Church, located at Eleventh and K Streets NW.

TO THE
CITIZENS OF WASHINGTON.

It is well known to you that events have transpired within the last few days, deeply affecting the peace and character of our community. The danger has not yet passed away, but demands increased vigilance from the friends of order.

The cool, deliberate judgment of the People of this community, unexceptionably and unequivocally declared, can, and will, we doubt not, if the Law is found insufficient, redress any grievance, in a manner worthy of themselves; but the fearful acts of lawless and irresponsible violence can only aggravate the evil.

The authorities, Municipal and Police, have thus far restrained actual violence; and they now invoke the citizens of Washington to sustain them in their further efforts to maintain the peace and preserve the honor of the city.

The peace and character of the Capital of the Republic *must* be preserved.

The Mayor of the City (confined to his bed by sickness) fully concurs in the above.

W. LENOX, *Pres. Board of Aldermen,*
J. H. GODDARD, *Capt. Auxiliary Guard.*
April 20, 1848.

The 600 block of F Street as it looked in the early 20th century. The former Patent Office, now the Smithsonian's National Portrait Gallery and American Art Museum, is in the background.

Broadside calling for citizens to remain calm following the attempted escape of 77 African American slaves aboard the *Pearl*.

Harriet Beecher Stowe by Alanson Fisher, 1853.

In 1851, from a new office one block south of here, the *National Era* began to serialize a novel by little-known author Harriet Beecher Stowe: *Uncle Tom's Cabin*. The publication of this powerful story intensified emotions on all sides and was pivotal in moving the country toward war.

There is modern civil rights history in this block, too. In the 20th century, Charles Hamilton Houston, an African American law professor at Howard University and a practicing attorney, had his law office at 615 F Street. Houston mentored the young Thurgood Marshall here and at Howard University. Later a Supreme Court justice, Marshall credited Houston with laying the groundwork for the modern civil rights movement by teaching him the strategies that overturned the doctrine of "separate but equal" facilities in schools in the 1954 landmark case, *Brown v. Board of Education.* ➤

.4

Charles Hamilton Houston, above, mentored future Supreme Court Justice Thurgood Marshall, left.

In the early 1950s, pickets at the corner of Seventh and F Streets demanded that the Hecht Company, once located in the building on the southeast corner, desegregate its lunch counter. This was part of a successful citywide campaign that resulted in a 1953 Supreme Court decision outlawing racial discrimination in public accommodations in Washington, D.C.

Belva Ann Lockwood lived in the 600 block of F Street, in one of the buildings pictured on the top of page 25. In the 1880s, she twice ran for president on the Equal Rights Party ticket. She was also the first woman to argue a case before the Supreme Court. In 1893, the Capitol Savings Bank opened in this same block to provide African American businessmen with financial resources frequently denied them by white banks.

MCI Center, home to
the Washington Capitals,
Washington Wizards, and
Washington Mystics,
seats 20,000 spectators.

Richard Busch

Former Hecht Department Store
Southeast corner, Seventh and F Streets NW

This building, formerly the home of the Hecht Company, is a typical white terracotta "palace of commerce." The Hecht Company of Baltimore first rented space in 513 Seventh Street in 1896, expanded into 515, built 517 in 1903, and then in 1924 had Jarvis Hunt design the larger corner building with elaborate decorative details. The Hecht Company marked the busy intersection with the clock that you can still see on the corner of the building. The Hecht Company is now located at Thirteenth and G Streets.

MCI Center
Northeast corner, Seventh and F Streets NW

Designed by Ellerbe-Becket of Kansas City and KCF/SHG and Devrouax & Purnell of Washington, D.C., this block-long, modern sports arena has settled into a neighborhood of more traditional urban architectural styles. Opened in 1997, it occupies more than a city block, extending across the former 600 block of G Street. The architects used setbacks and varied its façades to help mask the building's size. Each of the four façades is different, with the north end embellished with Asian-inspired motifs in a salute to the Chinatown neighborhood.

The west side of the 700 block of Seventh Street NW

Across the street and one block farther to the north of this intersection stands one of the finest intact post-Civil War blocks in downtown Washington. Once an integral part of a thriving German immigrant neighborhood, these commercial buildings fell on hard times over the years as businesses moved elsewhere. In 1999–2000, Douglas Development Corporation restored the entire block to look as it did during the late 19th century. Commercial uses are returning at street level, and offices now occupy the upper floors where 19th-century shop owners and their families lived.

▶ *Cross Seventh Street and follow F Street to the next trail sign, near Eighth Street, in front of the National Portrait Gallery.*

.5

Abraham Lincoln Walked Here

You are standing in one of Washington's best-preserved 19th-century streetscapes. The two grand Greek Revival-style buildings that face each other across F Street were begun in the 1830s, the first major federal buildings to be constructed after the White House and the Capitol. Originally the General Post Office and the Patent Office, they dominated a neighborhood of homes and small shops, and would turn this section of the city into a center of employment for lawyers and government clerks.

The Civil War dictated emergency uses for many government buildings, including these two. The Post Office became a commissary, and the Patent Office served initially as a place for the First Rhode Island Regiment to bunk upon its arrival in the city in 1861. Later, hospital beds for more than 2,000 Union soldiers, wounded at the battles of Second Bull Run, Antietam, and Fredericksburg, were lined up amid the patent-display cases.

President Lincoln passed this way often on his way through the city. In March of 1865, he and Mrs. Lincoln walked where you stand on their way to his second inaugural ball. The scene in the Grand Hall of the Patent Office was transformed from the misery of a makeshift hospital to the splendor of this inaugural event, where Mrs. Lincoln, elegantly gowned, and the president, looking tired and gaunt, celebrated with some 4,000 guests. When the crowd descended on banquet tables set for 300 at a time, the result was bedlam — broken china and glass and spilled food and drink. Just a few weeks later, the street rang with the hoofbeats of John Wilkes Booth's horse carrying Lincoln's assassin away from Ford's Theatre, a short two blocks away.

The Patent Office, about 1846.

"I have been up to look at the dance and supper-rooms, for the inauguration ball at the Patent office; and I could not help thinking, what a different scene they presented to my view a while since, fill'd with a crowded mass of the worst wounded of the war. . . .

To-night, beautiful women, perfumes, the violins' sweetness, the polka and the waltz; then the amputation, the blue face, the groan . . . and overall lay the heavy smell of putrefaction and death."

Walt Whitman, March 1865

The celebrated poet Walt Whitman, who nursed the wounded and also attended the inaugural ball, witnessed it all. His keen eye did not miss the stark contrast between the suffering and death in this temporary hospital and the elegance of the ball. ➤

The poet Walt Whitman as he looked in 1860 when photographed by Mathew Brady.

An engraving of the General Post Office from the corner of Eighth and E Streets NW, about 1844

The Historical Society of Washington, D.C.

.5

Robert Mills

Library of Congress

Old Patent Office
North side, F Street between Seventh and Ninth NW

Built over a 39-year period between 1836 and 1875 in four separate phases, the old Patent Office fills two city blocks. Today, it houses the Smithsonian's National Portrait Gallery and American Art Museum, two of the greatest collections of American art in the nation. (Now closed for renovation.) Robert Mills, the architect of the Washington Monument and parts of the U.S. Treasury building, supervised the construction according to designs by Town and Elliot, and it is likely that he designed the portico (porch) that you see today. The commanding presence of the central F Street façade, the first to be built, was inspired by the

Parthenon. Made of sandstone from Aquia Creek in Virginia (as was the Capitol building), its pinkish tone sets it apart from the later sections constructed of white marble. A monumental staircase to the original main entrance on today's second floor was removed in 1936 when F Street was widened.

General Post Office Building
South side, F Street between Seventh and Ninth NW

Robert Mills also designed the southern half of this building (facing E Street), constructed between 1839 and 1844 for use by both the federal Post Office Department and the City Post Office. Thomas U. Walter, who also designed the current Capitol dome, completed the F Street portion of the Post Office building in 1855. This all-marble structure represents an early use of the Italian Renaissance palazzo form for a government building. At one time, the building housed the U.S. Tariff Commission.

The Vistas: A Legacy of Pierre L'Enfant

As you stand near the historic marker, looking down Eighth Street, notice the view to your right and left along F Street. At the end of your sightline to the east (left) is the monumental Union Station. To the west (right) is the 15th Street side of the U.S.Treasury building. Ahead of you, down Eighth Street, is the National Archives.

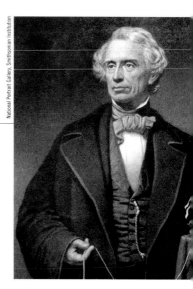

These vistas reflect the genius of Pierre L'Enfant, whose 1791 plan for the Federal City is one of the great design achievements in 19th-century America. The visual connections between distant parts of the city were central to his bold and visionary concept, which has remained relatively intact for more than 200 years.

Samuel F. B. Morse
by John Sartain.

First public telegraph

In 1845 the inventor and artist Samuel F. B. Morse opened and operated the first public telegraph in the United States from a building on the Seventh Street side of the General Post Office. (The telegraph line was owned by the federal government.) The telegraph was relatively new technology at the time of the Civil War, and it proved to be a valuable tool by which President Lincoln kept in touch with his generals throughout the country. A plaque commemorating Morse's activities can be found about mid-block on the Seventh Street side of the building.

LeDroit Building
Southwest corner, Eighth and F Streets NW

Designed in 1875 by James H. McGill, this fanciful structure was the first commercial building on what had been a residential block. Its architecture is Italianate, the most popular commercial style through the end of the 19th century. The large display windows on the second level, heavy brick hood moldings over the windows, and bracketed cornices are handsome architectural details.

Atlas Building
(also known as the Warder Building)
Southeast corner, Ninth and F Streets NW

Nicholas T. Haller was the architect for this 1892 structure, a strong, solid six-story Romanesque Revival early "skyscraper." One of its most interesting features is the use of bricks to create the patterned horizontal frieze at the top. The invention of elevators in the late 19th century made the construction of tall buildings practical for the first time.

● *Cross Ninth Street to the corner by the Courtyard by Marriott. The next trail sign is near the alley just past the hotel.*

.6

John Wilkes Booth's Escape

The alley near the trail sign has direct access to the rear of Ford's Theatre, just as it did on the night of April 14, 1865, when President Lincoln was shot there by John Wilkes Booth. The quotation to the right is the recollection of Henry Davis, who as a 12-year-old lived with his family in a house on Ninth Street NW. The Davis brothers would watch the goings-on behind the theater from the rear of their house. Henry went to bed early on April 14, leaving his brother to witness the dramatic events alone.

The nearby Courtyard by Marriott hotel on the southwest corner of Ninth and F is on the site of an earlier rooming establishment called Herndon House. Here, one of the Lincoln conspirators, Lewis Powell (also known as Lewis Paine and Lewis Payne), had a room. On the night of the assassination, Booth met here with the conspirators and made assignments: Powell was to kill Secretary of State Seward, co-conspirator George Atzerodt was to kill Vice President Johnson, and Booth took Lincoln for himself. Only Booth succeeded.

Booth injured his left leg when he jumped from the presidential box to the stage at Ford's after shooting the president. He limped to a horse he had waiting behind the theater, made his way along the alley system to F Street, and rode east on F on his flight to Virginia. There, in a tobacco shed, he was surrounded by federal soldiers. When it appeared that he was going to shoot his way out, Booth was himself shot and died shortly thereafter.

John Wilkes Booth as he looked about 1862.

An artist's rendering of Booth making his escape from the rear of Ford's Theatre.

"My brother saw Booth as he came down the alley and turned into F Street."

Henry Davis, 1902

Courtyard by Marriott
900 F Street NW

Before moving on, notice the imposing Romanesque Revival building at 900 F Street NW, originally a bank designed by James G. Hill in 1891. Its design marks a transition from the monumental classicism of the old Patent Office and old General Post Office to the commercial district west of Ninth Street. Its rugged granite Romanesque exterior belies the fact that it is a "modern" structure of steel and cast iron. The former main banking room is now the hotel's lobby, and its old vault has been incorporated into a restaurant.

Masonic Temple Building
901 F Street NW

Directly across F Street from today's Courtyard by Marriott is an example of a high-style Renaissance palazzo, marked by elaborate exterior ornamentation. It was designed by Cluss and Kammerhuber and built between 1867 and 1869 for the Masons, who have had a presence in the city since 1795. All early important government buildings had their cornerstones placed in a Masonic ceremony. Fifteen presidents of the United States were Masons, and one of them, former President Andrew Johnson, marched in the parade ➤

.6

that marked the opening of this building. Future president James A. Garfield was an active member of this lodge when he served as a U.S. Senator. The large two-story public space on the second floor (identified by the tall windows) was one of the most fashionable halls in the city, the site of numerous banquets and balls, including one for the then-Prince of Wales, the future Edward VII.

The building's exterior was restored in 1993 by Mary Oehrlein & Associates. Martinez & Johnson, architects, have designed a new building on Ninth Street that is linked to the old Masonic Temple by an atrium.

Ford's Theatre and a muddy Tenth Street the day after Lincoln's assassination.
The theatre and the Petersen House where the president died, are just around the next corner, to the left. Open to the public, both are well interpreted by the National Park Service.

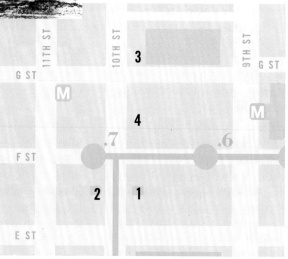

1 Ford's Theatre
2 Petersen House
3 First Congregational United Church of Christ
4 St. Patrick's Catholic Church

F Street, in the 1880s, looking west toward the Treasury. Herndon House where Booth and other conspirators met, is on left, where today's Courtyard by Marriott hotel stands. The Masonic Temple can be seen across the street.

Library of Congress

At the corner of Tenth and F Streets be certain to look to the right up Tenth for a view of two historic downtown church sites with strong ties to the Civil War era.

St. Patrick's Catholic Church
East side, Tenth Street between F and G Streets NW

Located a few steps north of F Street on the east side of Tenth is St. Patrick's Catholic Church, known as the "Mother Church of Washington" because it was the first church of any denomination founded (1794) within the boundaries of the City of Washington. Mary Surratt turned to St. Patrick's pastor, Father Jacob A. Walter, for guidance and spiritual comfort following her arrest and conviction for involvement in the assassination of President Lincoln. Father Walter, a staunch defender of Mrs. Surratt's innocence, walked with her to the gallows on July 7, 1865.

The cornerstone of the Gothic-style church you see today was laid in 1872.

First Congregational United Church of Christ
Northeast corner, Tenth and G Streets NW

Just a half-block farther, on the northeast corner of the next intersection (Tenth and G), is the First Congregational United Church of Christ, founded as First Congregational Church in 1865 on this site. One of its early leaders, Major General Oliver Otis Howard, had been chosen by President Lincoln to head the Freedman's Bureau, the federal agency dedicated to helping former slaves gain economic independence. In 1867, realizing the educational needs of African Americans, General Howard and other church leaders succeeded in getting congressional approval for establishment of a school open to all, including African Americans. Nearly all of the school's founders were members of First Congregational Church, and six of its early presidents were members, including General Howard. Because of the general's vision for the school, it was named Howard University.

❯ *Cross the intersection of Tenth and then cross F Street to the other side. Proceed to your left along F to the next trail sign in front of the former Woodward & Lothrop Department Store.*

.7

"Woodies" Comes
to F Street

From the 1880s to the 1950s, F Street was the heart of
Washington, D.C.'s downtown shopping district, and
Woodward & Lothrop, known to all as "Woodies," was
the grande dame of the department stores that anchored
it. The store operated on the corner of 11th and F for
almost 110 years, from 1887 until 1996.

It started with a Massachusetts businessman, Samuel
Woodward, who, like so many other entrepreneurs, saw
the promise of Washington, D.C., after the Civil War.
People were being drawn to the capital by new opportu-
nities, new federal jobs, and the grandeur of newly paved
broad avenues lit with gas lamps and lined with trees
— the result of a major modernization program in the
1870s led by Alexander Robey Shepherd, head of the
city's Department of Public Works. Horse-drawn public
streetcars, started during the Civil War, were carrying
people from their homes to a developing commercial
center downtown. Woodward came to the city to check
it out and wrote to Alvin Lothrop, his partner in the dry
goods business, "Washington, D.C., is the place for us."

"Woodies" main floor
awaits customers
in this holiday photo
from about 1950.

The Historical Society of Washington, D. C.

The founders of Woodward & Lothrop moved here from Boston in 1880, hence the name of their first store.

Woodward & Lothrop opened their Boston Dry Goods Store in 1880 near Center Market at Seventh Street and Pennsylvania Avenue. Seven years later they led the move of stores to F Street. Their modern establishment, now greatly expanded and called a department store, offered such innovations as a "one-price" policy, which meant the customer did not have to bargain with the clerk. Eventually other major retail institutions joined them on either end of the F Street shopping strip—Garfinckel's at 14th Street and the Hecht Company at Seventh.

Covering almost an entire city block, the Woodward and Lothrop building embodies the development of department stores as important urban institutions. The northern half, facing G Street, was designed by Henry Ives Cobb in 1902 and has fine terracotta and cast iron ornamentation, including medallions bearing the W&L monogram. The southern half facing F Street was designed by "Woodies" staff architect L.K. Ashford in 1927 to replace the series of old buildings that had housed the store since the 1880s. ➤

F Street and the Woodward
& Lothrop store during the
holidays in the late 1940s.

.7

An advertisement
showing Woodward
& Lothrop as the
retail center of the
nation's capital.

The Historical Society of Washington, D.C.

Other downtown entrepreneurs

Gustav Lansburgh came to the
capital from Baltimore in 1860 and
opened a store on nearby Seventh
Street. When Lincoln was assassinated
in April 1865, Lansbugh's sympathy
and his business acumen led him to
corner the market on black crepe,
needed by all to drape their buildings
in mourning. It made his name,
and his store became a landmark at
Seventh and E for the next hundred
years. (See page 23)

The Hecht Company anchored the
intersection of Seventh and F, and
was also entrepreneurial in bringing
to the city its first department store
exchange policy, the first use of
charge accounts, and the first escala-
tors. Although it was a latecomer
in 1896, it is the only 19th-century
Washington department store to
survive, now operating at Thirteenth
and G. (See page 27)

▶ *You now have two options:*

Conclude the Center Loop

Return to Tenth Street, see Ford's Theatre and the Petersen House, and then conclude your walk by proceeding down Tenth past the FBI Building almost to Pennsylvania Avenue. Cross Tenth to the opposite side, where you will find trail sign .8, highlighting Pennsylvania Avenue. This concludes the Center Loop.

Begin the West Loop

Continue along F Street to the corner of 13th. Turn right on 13th and walk one block to G Street. Cross G, turn left and cross 13th, and proceed to the next trail sign in front of The Church of the Epiphany, a few steps from the corner.

.8

Pennsylvania Avenue: Main Street for the City and the Nation

The great ceremonial way (just a few steps ahead) that today links the White House and the Capitol is a far cry from the country lane along which Thomas Jefferson rode to the White House following his inauguration in 1801. Then, the avenue was muddy when it rained, dusty when it was hot, and, in all seasons replete with ruts, holes, and tree stumps. Over its 200-year history, Pennsylvania Avenue has become our country's main ceremonial avenue, America's Main Street. It has been the inaugural route for every president since Jefferson.

When the Lincolns came to town in 1861, the street was lined with hotels, boarding houses, commercial establishments, and some residences. The president-elect left from Willards' Hotel and traveled along the avenue to his first inauguration. Mary Todd Lincoln shopped for goods and services for the White House at avenue stores. In April 1865, Lincoln's funeral cortege passed here. For two days in May 1865, it was the site of a grand review of victorious Union troops. The avenue has also been the parade route for suffragettes, civil rights advocates, champions of gay rights, anti-war protesters and the Ku Klux Klan, among many others seeking a national platform for their causes.

During the Civil War, the south side of the avenue, where the stately group of government office buildings known as the Federal Triangle now stands, was a dangerous and disreputable part of the city known as "Murder Bay." It was the site of gambling houses, saloons, cheap hotels, and houses of ill repute. It was also known as "Hooker's

Pennsylvania Avenue in 1861, looking toward the unfinished Capitol dome.

Mary Todd Lincoln as she looked during her White House years.

This invoice from a Civil War-era Pennsylvania Avenue store lists goods and services that Mrs. Lincoln bought for the Executive Mansion. The invoice bears her signature.

Department" because General Joseph Hooker tried to concentrate the activities of prostitutes in this area.

President John F. Kennedy is said to have commented on the shabbiness of the north side of Pennsylvania Avenue during his ride from the Capitol to the White House following his inauguration in 1961. The formation of the Pennsylvania Avenue Development Corporation (PADC), a quasi-governmental body, was one of the steps taken to redevelop that side of the street. Over the next three decades, the PADC provided physical improvements and encouraged the private sector to bring new office and commercial buildings as well as residences to the area. ➤

.8

Old Post Office Building
12th Street and Pennsylvania Avenue NW

Designed in the early 1890s in the then-popular Romanesque Revival style and constructed of rough-cut granite, the Post Office Building was the first federal building erected on Pennsylvania Avenue. Its style was soon out of favor, but it remained in place, serving its mission, while the classically inspired buildings of the Federal Triangle rose around it.

In the 1960s, the federal government planned demolition of the building in order to complete the Federal Triangle. Local citizens rallied to save it, and their success led to the formation of the citywide historic preservation organization, "Don't Tear It Down," now renamed the D.C. Preservation League. Plans developed by Arthur Cotton Moore/Associates in the early 1980s resulted in a successful and trend-setting adaptive reuse of the building for federal offices, shops, and a food court, all grouped around the original atrium. The 315-foot bell tower, the second tallest in the city, is open to the public.

Open 7 days a week. Call 202.606.8691 to verify hours: April – Labor Day: 8 am to 10:45 pm.
The day after Labor Day – April: 10 am to 5:45 pm
Restrooms are also available.

The Old Post Office Building as it looked while under construction in the early 1890s.

Library of Congress

By the early 1900s, Murder Bay had given way to many small businesses. This picture shows a livery stable at what was then 1405 E Street NW, the site of today's Department of Commerce and the White House Visitor Center. Through the gap at the top of the picture you can see a glimpse of the "new" Willard Hotel.

Evening Star Building
11th Street and Pennsylvania Avenue NW

This building at the northeast corner of 11th Street and Pennsylvania Avenue was built as a modern office and printing plant for the *Evening Star* newspaper in 1898. Its up-to-date design was meant to outshine the "old fashioned" design of the Post Office Building across the street. The *Evening Star* covered the city from 1852 until its purchase by the *Washington Post* in 1981, and was for many years Washington's leading daily newspaper.

FBI Headquarters
North side, 900 block of Pennsylvania Avenue NW

The monumental headquarters of the Federal Bureau of Investigation appeared on the avenue between 1967 and 1972. Its construction was part of a plan by the Pennsylvania Avenue Development Corporation to demolish and replace most of the 19th-century structures on the north side of the avenue with modern buildings. In the end, the FBI headquarters was the only one built. Security concerns in part dictated its closed appearance at the street level. Today, flags and trees are beginning to soften its presence. Its tours, featuring the crime-fighting prowess of FBI agents, continue to be among the most popular attractions for visitors to the city.

Hours: Mondays–Fridays 8:45 am to 4:15 pm
Closed all federal holidays.
Tour entrance: Ninth and E Streets

❑ *The Center Loop of the Downtown Heritage Trail concludes here. You may investigate more of downtown by following either or both the East and West Loops identified on the map in this booklet.*

The West Loop

THIS LOOP TAKES ABOUT 60 MINUTES to walk. Along the way you may visit The Church of the Epiphany, where the Jefferson Davises attended services before the Civil War; New York Avenue Presbyterian Church, where the Lincolns worshipped; and Asbury United Methodist Church, the oldest African American congregation in the city still located on its original site. You will pass the United States Treasury building, where the strategies that financed the Civil War were developed, and the Willard Inter-Continental Hotel, where Martin Luther King Jr., put the finishing touches on his "I Have A Dream" speech before delivering it at the Lincoln Memorial before a crowd of 200,000 in August 1963. The garden next to The Church of the Epiphany, and Pershing Park, across the street from the Willard, are pleasant places to rest. Shops, eating places, and street vendors abound along and near this loop.

W.1 The Church of the Epiphany

W.2 Franklin Square

W.3 Asbury United Methodist Church

W.4 New York Avenue Presbyterian Church at Herald Square

W.5 The United States Treasury

W.6 The Willard Inter-Continental Hotel

W.7 Freedom Plaza

W.1

The Church of the Epiphany

The Church of the Epiphany

The Reverend Charles H. Hall served Epiphany during the turbulent period in U.S. history from 1856 to 1869.

The Church of the Epiphany was one of eleven Washington churches that served as hospitals for Union wounded, and the only one downtown still standing. The Gothic Revival building dates back to 1844. Its original tower, built in 1857, was more slender than the one that exists today, which was erected in 1922.

In the years leading up to and during the Civil War, Washington was a city of strong Southern sympathies. Residents of the neighborhood around Epiphany reflected those feelings. During his career as secretary of war, congressman, and senator from Mississippi, Jefferson Davis and his family lived nearby and worshipped here. Epiphany's rector, Rev. Charles Hall, balanced his loyalties to the South with a strong Unionist stance, so much so that Lincoln's Secretary of War Edwin Stanton became a faithful parishioner, occupying the same pew that had been vacated by the Davis family, when Davis left to become president of the Confederacy. Many Union generals also attended this church.

Senators Judah P. Benjamin (Louisiana) and Robert Toombs (Georgia) lived one block over on F Street before becoming Davis's attorney general and secretary of state respectively. After Toombs left his residence at 1324 F Street NW, it became a boarding house. Union General Daniel Sickles recuperated here after being wounded at the Battle of Gettysburg, where he lost a leg. President Lincoln, surrounded by bodyguards, came here to visit his recovering general.

The Church of the Epiphany as it looked during the Civil War. New York Avenue Presbyterian Church, where the Lincolns attended, is in the background.

The Church of the Epiphany

In March 1862, before the church was converted into a hospital, President Lincoln, General George McClellan, the cabinet, members of Congress and the Supreme Court attended the funeral at Epiphany of General Frederick Lander, one of the first generals to die during the war.

Today, Epiphany is an active downtown parish and the venue for free Tuesday noontime concerts.

▶ *Return to the corner of 13th Street and proceed up 13th (to your left) about a block to the intersection with H Street and New York Avenue. To your left is New York Avenue Presbyterian Church. Cross H and the avenue and continue walking two more blocks to the next trail sign in front of the ornate Franklin School at 13th and K.*

Library of Congress

The 1400 block of F Street, above, was a fashionable residential neighborhood when Jefferson Davis and his wife Varina Howell Davis, right, attended Epiphany.

Library of Congress

W.2

Franklin Square

Pure water bubbled from a spring in this square in the early days of the city, when the area was far from the center of town. In the early 1830s, the fresh spring water was piped to the White House, the first running water to supply the executive mansion. People then called this place Fountain Square.

The area north of the square, while pastoral, had begun to develop into a fashionable residential area in the years immediately prior to the Civil War. However, it became decidedly less tranquil in 1861 when Union soldiers from the 12th New York Infantry Regiment filled the grassy expanse with tents and the sound of drill commands.

From time to time, President Lincoln could be seen in the neighborhood parked in an open carriage, surrounded by a few cavalrymen, conferring with Secretary of War Edwin M. Stanton, who lived at 1323 K Street on the north side of the square. When the president drove away, his eyes were sometimes drawn to soldiers playing baseball in the square.

The 12th New York Infantry Regiment drilling in Franklin Square, June 1861.

Library of Congress

By the late 1880s, fine townhouses lined 14th Street facing Franklin Square.

Later, African Americans made the square the rallying point for their annual Emancipation Day celebrations. District slaves were freed by act of Congress on April 16, 1862, eight months before the Emancipation Proclamation. This celebration by the "first freed" continued until the 1890s and has been recently revived in another location.

After the war, other prominent Washingtonians followed Secretary Stanton's lead in finding this remote section on the northern edge of the city a pleasant place to live. It was the equivalent of moving to the suburbs. When Secretary of the Treasury John Sherman and his wife moved to this block in the late 1870s, she told her friends they were "going into the country." Among the other elites living on the block or nearby were the Japanese and Russian ministers to the United States, and a future U.S. president, James A. Garfield. ➤

W.2

Franklin School
13th Street NW, east side of the square.

Today the elegant Franklin School is all that remains to remind us that this was once a fine residential neighborhood. Completed in 1869 according to designs by German-born Washington architect Adolph Cluss, the school won acclaim at the Paris Exhibition of 1878 for its modern facilities and fine architecture — a combination of Victorian Gothic, Romanesque Revival, High Victorian, and Second Empire. The building awaits a new use.

Alexander Graham Bell conducted sound experiments via light waves between the top of Franklin School and his nearby laboratory on L Street. Bell was excited about the

Library of Congress

Alexander Graham Bell

Charles Sumner School Museum & Archives

Franklin School as it looked about 1870. There were separate entrances for girls and boys.

One Franklin Square with its signature twin towers.

experiments and said he had "heard articulate speech produced by sunlight." His experiments were the beginning of wireless communications, although no practical result came of them until the more recent inventions of lasers, ultra-transparent glass fibers, and other developments in telecommunications.

What was once a fashionable residential neighborhood has become today an equally fashionable office-building enclave, its contemporary structures providing a foil to the 19th-century Franklin School.

One Franklin Square
K Street between 13th and 14th NW

Hartman-Cox, architects, designed this building to command the high ground on the north side of the square. Its twin towers, visible for miles around, were inspired by the landmark Art Deco Tower Building at 14th and K.

1300 I Street NW
Southwest corner, 13th and I Streets

Philip Johnson designed this "skyscraper" on the south side of the square. Johnson is the internationally renowned architect of the Glass House in New Canaan, Connecticut, as well as landmark skyscrapers across the country.

1225 and 1350 I Street NW
Northeast corner, 13th and I, and mid-block I Street, between 13th and 14th (respectively)

These two structures were designed by the Weihe Partnership to take advantage of the park: 1225 with a zigzag façade to provide an oblique view of the square, and 1350 with expanses of glass to reflect the greenery (in season).

> *Turn right at the corner of K Street and walk two blocks until you come to the next trail sign at Asbury United Methodist Church on the corner of 11th.*

W.3

926 11TH STREET NW, AT THE CORNER OF K STREET

Asbury United Methodist Church

Asbury United Methodist Church is the only African American congregation in the District of Columbia still occupying its original site. Founded in 1836 by 75 men and women — free and slave — from Foundry Methodist Church, Asbury's first sanctuary was surrounded by open land. The congregation's origins date to 1829, when the Rev. John F. Cook established the Asbury Sunday School in a building at 14th and H Streets. Rev. Cook also established Asbury's leadership position in education for youth by opening a public "colored" school at the church in 1836.

The Gothic Revival style church you see today dates from 1915. Built of Port Deposit (Maryland) granite, the stones came from the same quarry that provided the building blocks for present-day Foundry Methodist Church on 16th Street NW. The sanctuary seats 1,800 and is graced by the Good Shepherd Window, dedicated in 1915 to all the ministers who had served the church.

By the time of the Civil War, Asbury was a congregation of about 600, the largest of 11 black churches in the city. Its leadership, however, came from the Foundry Methodist congregation, and remained white until the Emancipation Proclamation was issued in 1863. The number of black churches in Washington at the time of the war reflects the District's large African American population, a strong presence since the city's founding

This building, constructed about 1836, was Asbury's first sanctuary. The congregation bought the lot at the corner of 11th and K Streets for $300.

Asbury members Mary Jane and Emily Catherine Edmonson (also spelled Edmondson) were aboard the ship *Pearl* in 1848, when it tried to spirit 77 African American slaves from the District to freedom. Descendants of the Edmonsons are members of Asbury today.

in 1800 when blacks made up 29% of the population. By 1830, a majority was free, and by 1860, free blacks owned property in every quadrant of the city.

Asbury symbolizes the struggle for freedom by African Americans and the visionary leadership of black clergy and congregations citywide. Asbury's members have played leading roles in the life of the city for more than 150 years. Civil rights activist Mary Church Terrell attended services at Asbury. Mary McLeod Bethune, the noted black educator, activist, and federal agency head during the administration of President Franklin Delano Roosevelt, was a church member. The late Patricia Roberts Harris, secretary of housing and urban development in the administration of President Jimmy Carter, attended Asbury. The church's education outreach efforts, begun by Rev. Cook, continue to the present day. ➤

W.3

Walk down 11th Street (along side Asbury's education building) on your way back to New York Avenue. The former Greyhound Bus Station is on the opposite side of the avenue at 1100.

1100 New York Avenue NW

This building stands as testament to the successful outcome of a lengthy battle waged by preservationists to save an historic Art Deco design long hidden and almost forgotten. The original bus terminal, designed in 1939 by Wischmeyer, Arrasmith & Elswick of Louisville, epitomized the era's streamlined Moderne style. It was "modernized" in 1976 by being encased in a covering of indifferent design that did, however, preserve the original architecture beneath. The terminal closed in 1987.

Preservation advocates first had to
pioneer the concept of landmarking
a structure that could no longer
be seen and then insist on new
construction that would adapt its
distinctive features to a new commercial use. The first 42 feet of
the terminal remain, meticulously
restored, and serve the new office
tower as lobby and storefronts.
Inside, a former ticket counter has
been adapted for use as an information desk, and other displays
around the lobby, which is open
on weekdays, evoke the building's
earlier use.

◐ *Now you are ready to walk back
along New York Avenue toward 15th
Street, where you come to New York
Avenue Presbyterian Church. The next
trail sign is on the New York Avenue side
of the church near the hitching post
where the Lincolns' horse and carriage
were tied while they attended services.*

W.4

New York Avenue Presbyterian Church at Herald Square

A smaller church similar in style to today's New York Avenue Presbyterian Church existed on this site at the time of the Civil War. It was here that President Lincoln and his family worshipped regularly from a pew selected by Mrs. Lincoln. That pew was saved when the original building was demolished in the early 1950s and may be seen in the church today. The president also attended mid-week prayer meetings at the church, sitting in an adjacent room with the door ajar so that he could listen without disturbing the gathering with his presence.

During the war, this church, like many others in the city, was slated for use by federal troops. The president heard the news one Sunday morning while attending services. From his pew, he decreed that this one would remain open, saying that, "the Churches are needed as never before for divine services."

The church's pastor, Dr. Phineas D. Gurley, served as Lincoln's personal spiritual guide. He was a frequent visitor to the White House, comforted the Lincolns on the death of their young son, Willie, and was one of several ministers who took part in funeral services in the East Room for the president himself. The church has on display an 1862 document in Mr. Lincoln's handwriting considered to be an early draft of the Emancipation Proclamation, which, when it was issued in January 1863, freed all slaves in the Confederacy. ➤

New York Avenue Presbyterian Church as it looked when the Lincolns attended services. The photo provides a glimpse of the surrounding residential neighborhood.

National Archives

National Portrait Gallery, Smithsonian Institution/ Gift of Mr. & Mrs. Timothy J. Desmond

1864 lithograph of the Emancipation Proclamation and President Lincoln by Albert Kidder.

President Lincoln and his family by William Sartain: (l to r) Tad, the president, Robert, and Mrs. Lincoln. A portrait of son Willie is on the wall in the background.

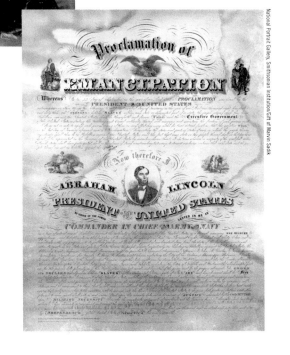

National Portrait Gallery, Smithsonian Institution/Gift of Marvin Sadik

© Bettmann/CORBIS

Eleanor Medill "Cissy" Patterson.

W.4

The Herald Building
1307 New York Avenue NW

The white, nine-story building near the corner of New York Avenue and 13th Street, was once the home of the *Times-Herald* newspaper, led by legendary publisher Eleanor Medill "Cissy" Patterson. The square takes its name from this paper.

In 1930, newspaper magnate William Randolph Hearst, owner of both the *Washington Times* and the *Washington Herald,* chose Patterson, daughter of a wealthy Chicago newspaper family, to edit the latter, an amazing accomplishment for a woman at the time.

Patterson quickly made the *Herald* the paper with the largest circulation and readership in Washington with innovations that included the first women's page. In 1939, she bought both papers, consolidated them into the *Times-Herald,* and initiated the first "round-the-clock" newspaper, foreshadowing the 24-hour news coverage of today's media. Patterson was a businesswoman, socialite, and political activist, a dominant force in the city's political and social life until her death in 1948. The *Times-Herald* was eventually acquired by the *Washington Post.*

National Museum of Women in the Arts
1250 New York Avenue NW

To the east where New York Avenue meets 13th and H Streets is the National Museum of Women in the Arts. Founded in 1981, following an international campaign, this museum is the first art museum in the world to be dedicated to works by women.

The museum is housed in the former Masonic Grand Lodge of the National Capital, designed by the Washington firm Wood, Donn & Deming in 1907. The Masons moved here when they outgrew their F Street location. (See page 33) The building's classic brick and limestone façades are a commanding presence in the neighborhood. Keyes Condon Florance, architects, converted it to museum use in 1987.

Hours: Weekdays and Saturdays, 10 am to 5 pm. Sundays, Noon to 5 pm.

Inter-American Development Bank
1300 New York Avenue NW

The Inter-American Development Bank was founded in 1959 to accelerate economic and social development in Latin America and the Caribbean. It invests in development projects and provides technical assistance for the preparation, financing, and implementation of development projects. The bank's Cultural Center features art exhibits and is open Mondays through Fridays from 11am to 6 pm.

The massive building, designed in 1983 by Skidmore, Owings & Merrill, gracefully acknowledges an awkward corner where H Street meets the avenue. An early example of Postmodern Classicism, an effort to use traditional design elements to relieve the austerity of contemporary buildings, it complements the National Museum of Women in the Arts.

● *Continue along New York Avenue toward 15th Street and the U.S. Treasury. Cross 15th Street, turn left and walk one-and-a-half blocks to the next trail sign.*

W.5

The United States Treasury

From an ornate office in the southeast corner of this building, President Lincoln's Secretary of the Treasury Salmon P. Chase developed the strategies that raised nearly $2.7 billion to finance the federal government and the Union war effort. He issued short- and long-term bonds, created paper money called "greenbacks," instituted internal revenue taxes, and created the first personal income tax in the United States. At the same time he unified the country's banking system to provide financial stability. It was an unparalleled feat. Shortly after Chase's resignation from the Treasury in 1864, President Lincoln appointed him Chief Justice of the Supreme Court.

The monumental Treasury building was constructed over a period of 34 years from 1836 to 1869. Robert Mills, architect of the Washington Monument and other major government buildings, conceived the design and began its implementation. Thomas U. Walter, Ammi B. Young, Isaiah Rogers, and Alfred B. Mullett all executed later portions of the building, using Mills's original design as their guide. The building's most outstanding feature is its 466-foot-long Ionic colonnade along 15th Street, which projects a powerful sense of structure and form that is the essence of Greek Revival architecture.

The U.S. Treasury building blocks the direct vista that Washington city planner Pierre L'Enfant envisioned between the Capitol and the White House. Folklore attributes the building's location to President Andrew

The Treasury building's north front under construction in 1867.

Jackson, who, to settle an ongoing dispute in Congress over its site, walked out of the White House one day in 1836, stuck his cane in the ground, and said "Put it here!"

In 1863, this building witnessed the final act in the history of African American slavery in the District of Columbia. Local slave owners who had demonstrated their loyalty to the Union came here to be paid in cash for their slaves, freed by President Lincoln in April 1862 in the only instance of compensated emancipation ever to be carried out anywhere in the nation. ➤

Reservations to tour the U.S. Treasury building may be made by calling 202.622.0896 or 202.622.0692 (TDD). To learn more about the building's architecture, visit the Curator's Home Page at www.ustreas.gov/curator.

W.5

Secretary of the Treasury Salmon P. Chase, whose restored office is seen above, is pictured "bleeding" funds from a willing United States in an 1862 cartoon at right.

"Lady clerks" leaving the Treasury building after a day's work trimming "Greenbacks." Manpower shortages during the Civil War led to the first employment of large numbers of women in the federal government.

Hotel Washington
15th Street and Pennsylvania Avenue NW

Before you cross 15th Street again to get to Pennsylvania Avenue, notice the building on the corner, the Hotel Washington.

A rooftop garden with fine views tops this Italian Renaissance palazzo-style hotel, a Washington landmark since 1917. The building's brick mid-section is embellished by a decoration called *sgraffito* made by applying white plaster over red and then scraping away the design. The building, designed by Carrere and Hastings, had its exterior decoration restored in 1985.

▶ *Cross 15th Street to the Hotel Washington and walk along Pennsylvania Avenue past the Willard Inter-Continental Hotel. The next trail sign is located on the 14th Street side of the hotel.*

Blanche K. Bruce, born a slave in 1841, and elected senator from Mississippi during Reconstruction, served as the first African American Register of the Treasury between 1881 and 1885, appointed by President James A. Garfield.

W.6

1401 PENNSYLVANIA AVENUE NW

The Willard Inter-Continental Hotel

There has been a hotel on this site since 1816, and one with the name Willard since about 1850. This hotel has hosted every U.S. president since Franklin Pierce visited in 1853. The American writer Nathaniel Hawthorne, while covering the Civil War for *The Atlantic Monthly,* captured its importance this way:

"This hotel, in fact, may be much more justly called the center of Washington and the Union than either the Capitol, the White House, or the State Department.

...You exchange nods with governors of sovereign States; you elbow illustrious men, and tread on the toes of generals.

...You are mixed up with office seekers, wire pullers, inventors, artists, poets... until identity is lost among them."

Nathaniel Hawthorne, about 1863

The Historical Society of Washington, D.C.

Hacks waiting in front of Willards' as it looked in 1861. The Treasury is in the background.

President-elect Lincoln arrived at Willards' Hotel at 6:30 am on February 23, 1861, under heavy security because of threats on his life. (His security detail was headed by Alan Pinkerton.) Lincoln and his family stayed there for ten days prior to his inauguration on March 4.

A peace conference attended by representatives from 21 of the 34 states took place at Willards' in February 1861, and was in session when the Lincolns arrived. It was a final attempt to avert war.

General Ulysses S. Grant checked into the hotel on March 8, 1864, with his 13-year-old son. He signed in "U.S. Grant and son," and then walked over to the White House to see the president. What military general today would arrive at a hotel unannounced and without a phalanx of aides? Later, as president, Grant popularized the word "lobbyist." After a day in the White House, Grant frequently enjoyed relaxing with a brandy and cigar in the Willards' lobby. As word spread about this nightly ritual, many people congregated there, waiting to approach him about their causes. Grant called them "lobbyists" and the label has remained. ➤

W.6

Willard Inter-Continental Hotel

Restored facade and
lobby of today's Willard
Inter-Continental Hotel.

Willard Inter-Continental Hotel

The Willard Inter-Continental Hotel of today is a Beaux-
Arts building designed in 1901 by Henry Hardenburgh,
who was also architect of the Plaza Hotel and the original Waldorf-Astoria in New York City. The Willard
closed in 1968 and stood empty and deteriorating until
1984, when a $120 million renovation, executed by
Vlastimil Koubek, architect, brought it back as a center
of Washington social activity.

Peace conference
delegates meeting
at Willards'
in February 1861.

Julia Ward Howe
(by Elliot & Cotton)
composed the words
to *The Battle Hymn
of the Republic*
at Willards' in 1861.

Pershing Park

Across the avenue is a shady oasis
designed in 1981 by M. Paul Friedberg
and Jerome Lindsey. The park
commemorates World War I hero
General John Pershing. Trees, greenery, and the sound of falling water
or the sight of ice skating in winter
provide a welcome respite from the
monumental buildings and bustle
of the surrounding area.

● *Cross 14th Street and walk straight
ahead along E Street. Cross 13th where
you will see the next trail sign on the
corner near the Warner Theatre.*

W.7

Freedom Plaza

Freedom Plaza, seen just across E Street diagonally from this sign, was so named in the 1980s to honor the memory of Martin Luther King, Jr., and his contribution to civil rights in the United States. King finished work on his "I Have A Dream" speech in a suite at the nearby Willard Hotel before delivering this major civil rights statement from the steps of the Lincoln Memorial before a crowd of 200,000 on August 28, 1963. It was the culmination of the "March on Washington for Jobs and Freedom."

Freedom Plaza also pays tribute to Major Pierre Charles L'Enfant, the young French military officer who served on General George Washington's staff at Valley Forge, and who, in 1791, designed the original plan for the City of Washington. A partial image of that plan is inscribed on the plaza's surface, and its manifestation can be seen in the street pattern and major public buildings visible from here today. (L'Enfant is buried in Arlington Cemetery in front of Arlington House.)

Freedom Plaza is an adaptation of a 1981 design by Venturi, Rauch and Scott Brown. The site of many hometown celebrations and annual events, the plaza is the place where nation's capital meets local city. ➤

Martin Luther King, Jr.
at the Lincoln Memorial
on August 28, 1963.

"I have a dream."

Martin Luther King, Jr., August 1963

Pierre L'Enfant's
visionary 1791 plan for
the City of Washington
(seen here in an 1800
version) remarkably
remains, almost entirely
intact, more than 200
years later.

W.7

National Theatre

The National Theatre, above, at the time of the Civil War.

President and Mrs. John F. Kennedy, right, entering the National Theatre to attend a performance.

Washingtoniana Division, D.C. Public Library

Max Hirshfeld

The late John A. Wilson, Chairman, Council of the District of Columbia.

National Theatre
1321 E Street NW

The National Theatre, on E Street facing Freedom Plaza, has presented live theater on this spot since 1835. Rebuilt many times to meet the tastes of new generations, the historic "Theatre of Presidents" has entertained every first family since its doors opened. President Lincoln and his family attended this theater many times, and on the evening of the president's assassination at Ford's Theatre, his son Tad was attending a performance here.

John A. Wilson Building
1350 Pennsylvania Avenue NW

On the opposite side of Pennsylvania Avenue from Freedom Plaza is the seat of District of Columbia government, the John A. Wilson Building, named for the late chairman of the D.C. Council. Designed in 1904 by Cope and Stewardson of Philadelphia, and known until recently as the District Building, its many embellishments identify it as an example of American Beaux-Arts Classicism.

In this building, three commissioners appointed by the president of the United States governed the city until 1974, when residents fought for and regained the right to elect their mayor and city council, denied them 100 years earlier. The building stands as the major symbol of the local city amid the commanding presence of the federal government.

Ronald Reagan Building and International Trade Center
1300 Pennsylvania Avenue NW

Located across Pennsylvania Avenue to the left of the John A. Wilson Building, this structure, with 3.1 million square feet, is the second largest federal office building in the United States. Only the Pentagon is larger in size. Designed by Pei Cobb Freed & Partners, it was constructed in the early 1990s and completes the government office complex known as the Federal Triangle. The building contains a Visitor Center and gift shop, a food court, and restrooms.

● *This completes the West Loop of the Downtown Heritage Trail. If you have not explored the Center and East Loops of the trail, use the map to lead you to these other parts of the downtown neighborhood.*

The East Loop

ALONG THIS APPROXIMATELY 60-MINUTE walk, you will see Washington's Old City Hall, the only place in the United States where President Lincoln's plan for compensated emancipation was carried out. You may visit the National Building Museum, housed in a structure modeled after an Italian palazzo and built to house the administration of Civil War pensions. Nearby is the Small Jewish Museum, housed in the city's oldest synagogue. The museum is open for tours and is located in a neighborhood of churches and former synagogues that evoke a time when many immigrant communities called downtown home. This part of the tour ends in Washington's Chinatown, where Mary Surratt's boarding house harbored some of the Lincoln conspirators. The colorful, grand Chinese archway greets you at Seventh and H Streets. The National Law Enforcement Officers Memorial across from the National Building Museum, and the garden of the Small Jewish Museum offer good resting places. The National Building Museum has a museum shop, café, and restrooms. Chinatown has many interesting restaurants.

e.1 Senator Daniel Webster

e.2 Old City Hall

e.3 The National Building Museum

e.4 Lillian and Albert Small Jewish Museum
Jewish Historical Society of Greater Washington

e.5 Mary Surratt's Boarding House

e.6 Chinatown

e.1

Senator Daniel Webster

Senator Daniel Webster of Massachusetts, one of the giants of American political history and an orator unmatched in his time, lived and worked in this block, in a house that once stood partly in the empty space next to 503 D Street, a pre-Civil War structure that closely resembles it. Webster believed fervently in the sanctity of the Union. In 1850, near the end of his life, he made his last great speech on the floor of the Senate in support of Kentucky Senator Henry Clay's plan to prevent the Union from breaking apart. That plan, known as the Compromise of 1850, put off the coming of war for another decade. Among its provisions was an end to slave trading in the District of Columbia.

Local courts have been in this area, known as Judiciary Square, since the earliest days of the city. It was also, in Webster's day, a fashionable residential neighborhood near Washington's City Hall, within walking distance of the Capitol. Magnificent Baptist, Episcopal, Methodist, and Unitarian churches, now all demolished, once commanded the neighborhood skyline.

Senator Daniel Webster on the floor of the U.S. Senate in 1830 delivering one of his great orations.

Library of Congress

Trinity Episcopal Church, designed by James Renwick, seen here in the 1860s, once stood on the northeast corner of Third and C Streets. Renwick was well known as the architect of the Smithsonian Castle. The Capitol dome is nearing completion.

D.C. Recorder of Deeds Building
515 D Street NW

Built on part of the Daniel Webster house site is the D.C. Recorder of Deeds building, designed in 1941 by municipal architect Nathan C. Wyeth in Art Deco style. The building has strong links to black history in the District of Columbia. In 1881, Frederick Douglass was appointed Recorder of Deeds. A former slave, who achieved his freedom before the Civil War, his writing and oratory on behalf of abolition and equal rights had made him the most influential African American of his day. For almost the next 100 years, the Recorder of Deeds position was the highest appointment for African Americans in the city. The building's lobby contains several large murals celebrating such prominent figures as Benjamin Banneker, the free African American mathematician and first African American man of science, who assisted Andrew Ellicott in surveying the original 10-mile-square federal district.

The Chase mansion, home to Lincoln's secretary of the Treasury, was located on the northwest corner of Sixth and E Streets. It was here that President Lincoln attended the 1863 wedding of Kate Chase to Senator William Sprague of Rhode Island.

● *Walk along D Street about half a block to the statue of Abraham Lincoln and the next trail sign in front of the former Superior Court of Washington, D.C. This building once served as Washington's City Hall. On your way, in the landscaped area to the left, you will pass a gilded sculpture that honors Joseph James Darlington, a distinguished member of the D.C. Bar who died in 1920. In this sculpture by Carl Paul Jennewein, the nymph turns to protect a weak and innocent faun.*

e.2

Old City Hall

This building, now a court building, began life as Washington's City Hall and was the first public structure erected in the District of Columbia for use by city government. Designed by George Hadfield (who also designed Arlington House, the Custis-Lee Mansion in Arlington Cemetery) and constructed between 1820 and 1850, the building is considered a fine example of the then-emerging Greek Revival style.

It housed the local court and elected city council and mayor of the District of Columbia until 1871, when the District briefly became a territory. In 1874, three commissioners appointed by the president of the United States began a 100-year system of government that lasted until "home rule" was partially reinstated in 1974.

One of the most important local events to take place here occurred in 1862. On April 16 of that year, President Lincoln had authorized up to $1 million to compensate loyal District of Columbia slave owners for their human property — eight months before the Emancipation Proclamation. A three-man Emancipation Commission, established by Lincoln, met here to interview each individual owner, examine their slaves, and assess the fairness of the owners' monetary claim. Assisting them was a slave trader from Baltimore who brought first-hand knowledge to the evaluation process. Enslaved African Americans, treated here as property, had played major roles in the early federal city. Some had helped build the Capitol and other federal buildings, others had held positions of high trust in the daily life of the city. ➤

D.C. City Hall as
envisioned by architect
George Hadfield.
This rendering includes
the dome that was
never built.

In the days before the
Civil War, this building,
located nearby at the
corner of Third Street
and Pennsylvania Avenue
NW, was known as the
St. Charles Hotel. Noted
for its hospitality to
slave owners, it con-
tained below-ground
holding pens where
slaves were confined
while their owners
enjoyed the comforts
of the hotel upstairs.

e.2

The first Lincoln
memorial in
the United States
once stood on
a 35-foot column.

Bronze sculptures anchor the National Law Enforcement Officers Memorial.

National Law Enforcement Officers Memorial

The memorial, dedicated in 1991 by President George H.W. Bush, honors the service and sacrifice of America's law enforcement professionals and pays tribute to those who lost their lives in the line of duty. Among the more than 15,000 names engraved on the memorial's "pathways of remembrance" are those of 29 officers who lost their lives during the Civil War. Associated exhibits are located at a visitors center at 605 E Street.

For additional information, call 202.737.3400 or visit the memorial's website at www.nleomf.com.

▶ *Walk through the memorial park to the opposite side (F Street), where you will find the next trail sign located on the sidewalk to your left near the corner of the park.*

First Lincoln Memorial

The statue of President Lincoln in front of the court building is the first public monument erected in memory of the assassinated leader. Designed by sculptor Lot Flannery, the marble memorial was dedicated in 1868, on the third anniversary of the former president's death. The memorial was paid for almost entirely by residents of the District of Columbia and originally stood atop a 35-foot column.

Continue past Old City Hall to the corner of Fourth Street. Turn left at Fourth and walk one block to the corner of E. Cross E, turn left again, and proceed to the middle of the block. You will be on the E Street side of the National Law Enforcement Officers Memorial.

e.3

● 401 F STREET NW

The National Building Museum

This extraordinary structure was constructed between 1882 and 1887 to house the Pension Bureau, whose enormous task it was to administer the pensions owed to Civil War soldiers, their widows and orphans. The Pension Bureau was a forerunner of today's Department of Veterans Affairs.

Designed by architect and engineer Major General Montgomery C. Meigs, Quartermaster General of the Union Army during the Civil War, the building is in the Italian Renaissance style and modeled after the Palazzo Farnese in Rome. It contains 15.5 million bricks and is enhanced by a terracotta frieze 3 feet high and 1,200 feet long running around the entire building between the first and second stories. The frieze depicts Civil War forces — infantry, cavalry, artillery, navy, quartermaster, and medical units — in 28 individual panels that create a continuous parade.

One of the building's most spectacular features is its Great Hall, approximately 300 feet long and 100 feet wide. It is separated into three areas by two rows of four massive Corinthian columns that support the central roof. Each individual column is 75 feet tall and is constructed of 70,000 bricks. This great interior space has been the site of 14 presidential inaugural balls since President Grover Cleveland held his there in 1885, even before the building was completed.

Library of Congress

Major General Montgomery C. Meigs. His only son, John, was killed in the Civil War. Some have called this building with its frieze, a memorial to all who served in the war, an equivalent of today's Vietnam Veterans Memorial.

The National Building Museum with the pool of the National Law Enforcement Officers Memorial, foreground.

The 1901 Inaugural Ball of President William McKinley was held at the Pension Building.

The structure now houses the National Building Museum, the only museum in America dedicated to achievements in architecture, urban planning, construction, engineering, and design. Exhibits highlight the history of the building as well as the development of the nation's capital. A museum shop, café, and restrooms are located inside.

Hours: Weekdays and Saturdays, 10 am to 5 pm. Sundays, Noon to 5 pm.

▶ *After you have completed your visit in this area, walk back along F Street about a block and a half to Third; turn left, and walk one block to the corner of Third and G Streets to the next trail sign near the Lillian and Albert Small Jewish Museum.*

e.4

Lillian and Albert Small Jewish Museum

Jewish Historical Society of Greater Washington

Downtown was home to immigrant communities from the earliest days of the city, when Irish and Germans recruited to help build the new government buildings settled here. Later, newcomers from Italy, Greece, Russia, and elsewhere chose to start stores and businesses in this area because it was close to the Center Market at Seventh and Pennsylvania. In the days before public transportation, shop owners lived over the store or close by, and others who worked in the neighborhood lived close enough to walk to work. Churches and synagogues served the spiritual needs of these communities and helped preserve their languages and customs.

Churches and former synagogues remaining in this downtown neighborhood today are both a legacy of 19th-century downtown immigrant communities and testaments to their adaptability to changing times and new religious uses. The Lillian and Albert Small Jewish Museum, the home of the Jewish Historical Society of Greater Washington, is one example. Built in 1876 at the corner of Sixth and G Streets NW, amid a thriving German Jewish neighborhood, it was home to Adas Israel Congregation, whose members favored a traditional Orthodox form of worship. President Ulysses S. Grant attended the synagogue's dedication ceremony. When the congregation outgrew this building in the early 1900s, it became a Greek Orthodox church and later served an evangelical congregation before becoming a carry-out restaurant. Today it stands in a new location as the city's oldest surviving synagogue building, and houses changing exhibits on the history of the Jewish community of Washington, D.C. ➤

Open Sundays through Thursdays, Noon to 4pm.

"The neighborhood
was our whole life."

Albert Small, born in the neighborhood in 1902

The Washington Post Company

When demolition
threatened the former
Adas Israel synagogue
in 1969, the Jewish
Historical Society of
Greater Washington
mobilized to have the
building moved to its
present location at
Third and G Streets NW.

e.4

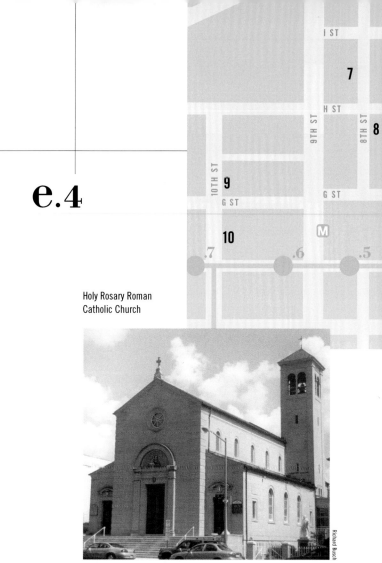

I ST

7

H ST

9TH ST

8TH ST

8

10TH ST

9

G ST

G ST

M

.7 .6 .5

10

Holy Rosary Roman
Catholic Church

Richard Busch

Downtown Religious Sites:
An Immigrant Legacy

A roll call of the churches
and former synagogues
in this area reflects the
waves of change in this
historic neighborhood.

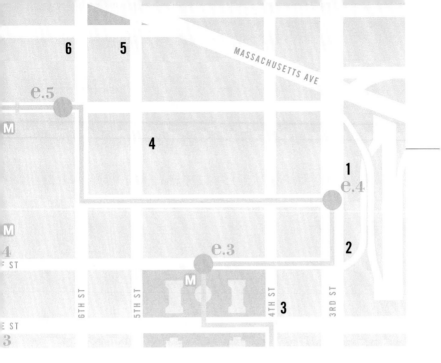

1 The Lillian and Albert Small Jewish Museum, in the city's oldest surviving synagogue, is described on page 82.

2 Holy Rosary Roman Catholic Church has been a presence in the neighborhood since 1913, when it was established to serve a nearby Italian immigrant community. The church you see today at 595 Third Street NW was built in 1927.

3 First Trinity Lutheran Church, 307 E Street NW, was established before the Civil War to serve German Lutherans. Its site was purchased in 1852 for 25 cents per square foot, and the cornerstone of the original church was laid in 1856. The current building was constructed in the early 1950s.

4 St. Mary Mother of God Catholic Church, Fifth and H Street NW, was originally founded in 1846 to serve German Catholics. Today one of its Sunday masses is in Cantonese. The current church building was built in 1890.

5 Corinthian Baptist Church, Fifth and I Streets NW, started out as the home of Assembly Presbyterian Church, the cornerstone of which was laid in 1852. In 1906, Assembly sold the building to Ohev Sholom Congregation, a Russian Jewish congregation, which replaced the steeple with a dome. Ohev Sholom was a neighborhood presence until 1956, when it sold the building to Corinthian Baptist. ➤

Turner Memorial
A.M.E. Church

Richard Busch

e.4

6 Turner Memorial A.M.E. Church, 600 I Street NW, is an African American congregation occupying the second home of Adas Israel Congregation. Built between 1906 and 1908, it served as a synagogue until its congregation moved to upper northwest Washington in 1951.

7 Greater New Hope Baptist Church, on Eighth between H and I Streets NW, was constructed in 1897 and 1898 on the foundations of a former Methodist church by the Washington Hebrew Congregation, the city's oldest Jewish congregation. It has been home to this African American church since 1955.

8 Calvary Baptist Church, on the corner of Eighth and H Streets NW, was established in 1862 by supporters of Abraham Lincoln and the abolition of slavery who had withdrawn from E Street Baptist Church because of its Southern sympathies. The cornerstone of the original church, designed by Adolph Cluss, was laid in 1864. That building burned during the winter of 1867. The present building, constructed in the same design, was completed in 1869.

Jack Boucher

St. Mary Mother of God
Catholic Church

9 First Congregational United Church of Christ, 10th and G Streets NW, was founded on this site in 1865 as First Congregational Church. Among its early members was former Civil War General Oliver Otis Howard, who headed the Freedmen's Bureau after the war and was instrumental in founding the school that became Howard University. President and Mrs. Calvin Coolidge attended services regularly at First Congregational during his tenure as chief executive in the 1920s. The current church building dates from 1961.

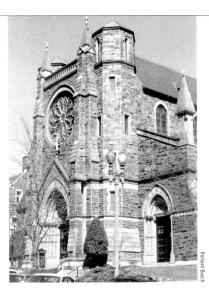

St. Patrick's Catholic Church

10 St. Patrick's Catholic Church, 10th and F Streets NW, was founded in 1794 to serve an Irish community and later welcomed Italians moving into the neighborhood into its congregation. It is known as the "Mother Church of Washington" because it was the first church of any denomination established within the original city limits. The current church building was constructed between 1872 and 1884 as funds were available.

❯ *From the Small Museum, walk west along G Street to Sixth and turn right. (The MCI Center is located on this block of Sixth Street.) Walk one block north on Sixth to H and turn left. This is Washington, D.C.'s Chinatown. The next trail sign is in front of 604 H Street, Golo's Restaurant.*

e.5

Mary Surratt's Boarding House

Mary Surratt moved to this house from southern Maryland following the death of her husband and took in boarders to help support herself. She was a pious Roman Catholic and a supporter of the Confederacy. Her son, John, had served the Confederacy as a spy and dispatch carrier. He was recruited by John Wilkes Booth, the dashing matinee idol of the day, who had a pathological hatred of President Lincoln, to take part in a conspiracy to assassinate the president and other high federal officials.

Booth, a member of a famous American theatrical family, visited the Surratt house on several occasions to see John and others associated with the conspiracy who stayed there. Booth and his fellow conspirators probably never had a formal meeting in Mrs. Surratt's house, but their occasional presence tied the house to the plot.

Three days after the assassination, Mrs. Surratt was arrested here through an unlucky set of circumstances. Just as federal officials who had questioned her were leaving, Lewis Powell (also known as Lewis Paine and Lewis Payne) came to the door. Powell had previously been identified as the man who had attempted to kill Secretary of State William Seward on the night of Lincoln's assassination. That was enough for the federal authorities to implicate Mrs. Surratt. She was taken into custody, given a military trial, and along with three of the conspirators (Lewis Powell, George Atzerodt, and David Herold), hanged on July 7, 1865, on the grounds of what is now Fort McNair in Southwest Washington. Her guilt remains a subject of debate.

Mary Surratt's boarding house at 604 H Street NW as it looked about 1910, in a quiet neighborhood of German immigrants.

Mary Surratt as she looked about the time of the Civil War.

Wah Luck (Chinese Happiness) House
Northwest corner, Sixth and H Streets NW

Designed by Chinese-born Washington architect Alfred Liu, this apartment building incorporates some Chinese detailing and has an Oriental garden in its small inner courtyard. It was built as part of an agreement between community leaders and the D.C. government to provide housing for older members of the Chinese community.

◗ *Continue along H Street toward the Chinese Arch spanning the street near the intersection with H. The next trail sign is just around the corner from the Metro entrance on Seventh.*

e.6

SEVENTH AND H STREETS NW

Chinatown

The colorful Chinese arch at the intersection of Seventh and H Streets NW stands in the heart of a small but vibrant Chinese community that thrives amid high-rise office development and an emerging downtown entertainment district. The arch, designed by Chinese-born Washington architect Alfred Liu, was a gift to Washington, D.C., from the city of Beijing, its sister city, which sent native craftsmen to help construct it in 1968. More than 280 dragons adorn the arch, ancient symbols of the spirits believed to bring rain and prosperity in China.

Washington's Chinese community first established itself in the 1880s on Pennsylvania Avenue NW, between Third and Four-and-One-Half Streets (now John Marshall Place). Restrictive immigration laws kept it a small bachelor community. Displaced by the construction of the Federal Triangle in the 1930s, the Chinese, not without protest from neighborhood residents, secured property along H Street in what was then a dwindling German immigrant community. The Chinese community renovated and redecorated the 19th-century residential

A dragon parade is part of the annual Chinese New Year's celebration.

Richard Busch

90

Chinatown
Friendship Archway.

buildings they found there to reflect its own history and culture. The long-time headquarters of the On Leong Chinese Merchants Association at 618 H Street NW, the organization that facilitated the move from Pennsylvania Avenue, recently became a restaurant.

During the 1950s and 1960s, many Chinese Americans chose to move to the suburbs, but the community is dedicated to preserving a slice of Chinese culture in this downtown location. The neighborhood has developed design guidelines for streetlights, sidewalk paving, and signs that reflect a Chinese influence and help reinforce the special character of the area. The Chinese New Year is celebrated here annually with a dragon parade and firecrackers, an event that draws increasingly large crowds from the entire metropolitan area.

This was once a largely German residential neighborhood. You can still sense its former residential character in the height and scale of some of the remaining buildings. The Surratt House at 604 H Street is one such example, and the small, recently restored building at 713 H Street in the next block is another. It dates from the 1840s and started life as someone's home. ➤

e.6

Calvary Baptist Church
Southeast corner, Eighth and H Streets NW

Calvary Baptist Church, one block farther along H Street at the corner of Eighth, has been a presence in the neighborhood since 1862. Civic leader Amos Kendall, who had been a member of President Andrew Jackson's cabinet, paid for the land and the building, envisioning a church open to all and deeply involved in the community. In 1889, Calvary recognized the growing Chinese population in the area and established a Chinese Sunday School for this community. Later, Calvary was instrumental in laying the groundwork for today's Chinese Community Church. Calvary was the church of Supreme Court Chief Justice Charles Evans Hughes and President Warren Harding.

Calvary Baptist Church, designed by Adolph Cluss, in an 1866 photo by Mathew Brady and, below right, decorated for a July Fourth holiday.

Calvary Baptist Church

Calvary Baptist Church

The 700 block of Seventh Street NW as it looked in the early 1900s. The west side of the block has recently been restored by the Douglas Development Corporation.

Greater New Hope Baptist Church and the Carnegie Library

To the north along Eighth Street NW is Greater New Hope Baptist Church, previously the home of Washington Hebrew Congregation. Beyond, located in the center of Mt. Vernon Square, is the Beaux-Arts-style Carnegie Library, a gift to the city from Andrew Carnegie in 1902. The city's central library for nearly 70 years, the building will open as the Museum of the City of Washington in 2003.

⬤ *This completes the East Loop of the Washington's downtown heritage trail. You may return to the Pennsylvania Avenue area by walking down Seventh, Ninth, or any numbered street.*

Bibliography

The sights and information highlighted along this walking trail and in the guidebook just begin to scratch the surface of the rich and multi-layered history of downtown Washington, D.C., at the time of the Civil War and after. For more information about the history of this neighborhood, please consult resources in the Washingtoniana Division, D.C. Public Library; the library of The Historical Society of Washington, D.C.; and any of the following works. For more Civil War sites in the city, see the brochure "Civil War Washington," available at the Visitor Center in the Ronald Reagan Building, 1300 Pennsylvania Avenue NW.

AIA Guide to the Architecture of Washington, D.C., 3rd Edition, Christopher Weeks, 1994.

Buildings of the District of Columbia, Pamela Scott and Antoinette Lee, 1993.

Capital Losses: A Cultural History of Washington's Destroyed Buildings, James M. Goode, 1979.

City of Magnificent Intentions, Keith Melder, 1983.

The City of Washington: An Illustrated History, The Junior League of Washington, 1977.

A Guide to Civil War Washington, Stephen M. Forman, 1995.

The Guide to Black Washington, Revised Edition, Sandra Fitzpatrick and Maria R. Goodwin, 1999.

Mr. Lincoln's City: An Illustrated Guide to the Civil War Sites of Washington, Richard M. Lee, 1981.

Mr. Lincoln's Washington, Stanley Preston Kimmel, 1957.

The Records of the Columbia Historical Society, 1895–1989.

Reveille in Washington, Margaret Leech, 1941.

The Sacrificial Years: A Chronicle of Walt Whitman's Experiences in the Civil War, edited with an introduction by John Harmon McElroy, 1999.

Testament to Union: Civil War Monuments in Washington, D.C., Kathryn Allamong Jacob, 1998.

The WPA Guide to Washington, D.C: The Federal Writers' Project Guide to 1930s Washington, Works Progress Administration for the District of Columbia, 1942.

Washington: A History of the Capital, 1800 - 1950, Constance McLaughlin Green, 1962.

Washington History, magazine of The Historical Society of Washington, D.C. 1989 – present.

Washington in Lincoln's Time, Noah Brooks, edited with an Introduction by Herbert Mitgang, 1958.

Worthy of the Nation: The History of Planning for the Nation's Capital, Frederick Gutheim, 1977.

ACKNOWLEDGMENTS

Civil War to Civil Rights exists because of the generous support of the Downtown DC Business Improvement District (BID). Deputy Director Joe Sternlieb and Transportation Coordinator Anne-Marie Bairstow were with us at every step of the project — and for the extra mile. The BID's generous investment in the Downtown Heritage Trail is another example of the organization's work to create a vibrant and inviting downtown, one that highlights the rich history of this neighborhood and that provides visitors and residents alike with interesting things to see and do.

Many others helped make this project a reality, including historians Professor Edward Smith (American University), Steve Hoglund, Keith Melder, Edwin C. Bearss (Historian Emeritus of the National Park Service), Ernest Furgurson, Aaron Lloyd, and architectural historian Linda B. Lyons. Special thanks go to the downtown stakeholders — representatives of the sites along the trail — for their comments and suggestions.

Diane Hamilton did the photographic research that made the stories come alive. Her knowledge of resources at the Library of Congress and the National Archives was invaluable. Mary Ternes, formerly of the Washingtoniana Division, D.C. Public Library, helped locate a number of specific photographs.

Susan L. Klaus, Jane Freundel Levey, and Barbara Wolfson edited the manuscript. Susan Klaus and Ann Goodman test-walked the trail.

Special thanks to Kathryn Schneider Smith, Executive Director of the DC Heritage Tourism Coalition, for her vision of this project, her knowledge of Washington history, and her unstinting gift of time and guidance that was always on the mark.